Life and Love, it's all about poetry

A Book of Poetry published by

MONTGOMERY
PRODUCTIONS

First printing

Life and Love, it's all about poetry,

Library of Congress Cataloging-in-Publication Data

ISBN 1-930576-00-5

Montgomery Productions
4919 Flatshoals Pkwy Suite #200 PMB152,
Decatur, GA 30034-5256
www.micmor@concentric.net

Printed in the United States of America
September, 2002

Book Cover illustration: Roderick Alexander
Montgomery Productions © 2002

Montgomery Productions

Presents

Life and Love,

It's all about poetry

By Michael Montgomery Matthews

This work is dedicated to my mother, for she is my inspiration and motivation. It is because of her that I have pushed to pursue my goals and my dreams. I also credit my family and my friends. They have been the constant support that I've needed to help me help myself, keeping me focused and determined. I owe my gratitude and my thanks to you all. This is only the beginning of a long road that I have started to travel on and it is because of your encouragement and belief that I will succeed.

Forward

Believe in yourself and the dreams that you have, for the journey of life can be long and very eventful with many changes along the way. Believe in those dreams with passion, for they are the unmistakable maps of life, which propel us to make it through. To live day to day with hope, that there is something better. Life is nothing more than poetry in its purest form. There are no real rules, only unpredictable artistry. That's where love fits into the massive puzzle. A natural beginning and end to all things.

Featured Poems

Phase One

Anything Goes

its all about poetry

My Love

Beauty is in the eye of the beholder,

but your beauty holds the world over,

your charm and grace,

opens my heart to that special place,

where only love is the key

that unlocks paradise for you and me...

Time is always endless when I'm in your presence,

and your love, your love is continuous,

a special love of tenderness,

given freely to me without reservation or hesitation,

you allow me to sip from the cup of your love that constantly overflows,

my heart is filled forever and a day,

for being with you is truly gratifying in every way...

I'm Just Passing Through

Through the days and through the nights,

I look and study the episodes of my life,

where I've been, the things I've done,

the places I've seen, the battles I've lost and won...

Always a clear reflection of the past and present,

shielding the direction of future,

the failure, the success,

decisions made, indiscretions, unfair play,

all resurfacing now, right in the middle of today...

Examining the do and don't, the right and wrong,

asking why and why not, always on and on,

never really knowing what it all means,

just passing through,

like something out of a dream...

Waiting

A long time coming,

you know it's true,

for I've waited and waited for you...

Plans, promises we've both made,

never following through,

only locking our feelings away, keeping them enslaved...

One thing or another,

it has always been,

never allowing spontaneous glee or blend...

Yet, I have held on all this time,

for it has been no doubt

that you would be mine...

So this is the day, the night, the right time,

when our hearts will come together,

just like rhythm and rhyme....

Love Hurts

Love hurts when you care so much,

it hurts when your love leads to mistrust,

it hurts in times of happiness,

when love reveals traces of sadness,

very seldom seen,

until love causes something cruel and mean...

Love hurts because of the heartbreak,

it hurts because you think you've made a mistake,

which leads you to believe that love is fake...

Love hurts when infidelity arises,

causing internal scars of enormous sizes,

it hurts in the reality you face,

leaving you searching for a state of grace...

Love's hurt will continue in this way,

until it is nurtured and cherished each and every day...

its all about poetry

Anticipation

Anticipation is what I feel,

as I attempt to earn your love,

frustration comes when there's no appeal,

when I know I am not the one you think of...

I look to find any way I can,

to show and prove to you I am your man,

but it seems my way is not the path,

that will lead my crusade for a love that I must have...

So I must find the key to your heart,

that will unlock the door of my dream,

and in the wake of my dream, I shall make my mark,

which is the mark of love and everything it means...

There is no doubt that we will be together,

for I will never stop in pursuit of your love,

because for me, there is no one better...

A Feeling

I have a feeling inside,

it tells me something about you,

a feeling that has been with me since we met,

as it is today, something special...

A warmth,

a closeness that's real,

things I would not have imagined,

things with sensual appeal,

everything I'd hoped for,

compassion, companionship and more...

Feelings that can't be explained,

but exists and will always remain,

for as long as you are with me,

filled with love is how I will always be...

Infidelity

Here I stand accused of being unfaithful,

told I value nothing, and never grateful,

a villain in cloths of black,

a dark night filled with indecent acts...

It's mystifying to me,

for these are things I cannot see,

my hideous and awful ways,

make me cruel,

labeled as nothing more than a common fool...

Tried, judged, and sentenced,

given the death penalty,

without a single witness,

guilty until proven innocent,

not the law of the land,

but in cases such as these,

it pertains to every woman and every man...

Defense,

no need to try,

because all that is said, will be considered a lie,

can there be justice or a truce,

using those immortal words,

" I didn't do it and that's the truth"...

An accusation everyone may face,

more than once in a lifetime,

being held accountable each and every time...

Holding You

Holding you is more than a simple pleasure,

it is a tranquility that can't be measured,

a moment of love and trust,

housing shades of erotic lust...

Beside you, lying still is more than a task,

for the warmth of your body creates anticipation

and brings sweet memories of the past...

The intimacy that exists,

is a heat that makes love-making hard to resist,

the knowing of your every desire,

moves my soul and sets my heart on fire...

A woman who will always be the center of all my fantasies,

I hold you now for today and tomorrow,

and all the wonderful nights that will follow...

Life and Love

Lost Love

When the stars come out and light up the night, my sadness comes,

because I know I've lost the love of my life...

When the wind blows it's chilling breeze,

my heart cries out,

for it no longer has the warmth and care it needs...

When the quiet rain comes down,

there's no peace in it's sound,

only the loud shattering of a broken heart,

falling to the ground...

When the morning sun rises there are no words to say,

only the hope, that my love shall return someday...

In Need of You

I wait and wait, until there can be no more,

the minutes, the hours, the days,

knowing it's your love that I wait for...

In the morning, through the night,

without you, time is a long burden,

and somehow it doesn't seem right,

loneliness was meant for no one,

but lonely is what I've become...

Sitting with my thoughts of you,

running round and round,

I feel like I can't make it,

on the verge of an emotional breakdown...

Something has to change,

for I can't endure this love pain,

so come to me, so I can be revived,

my body awakened and my spirit alive...

A Lady

Sitting on the grass sweet as a daisy,

was the prettiest, peaceful looking lady,

her head buried deep inside of a book,

she projected the most wonderful innocent look...

She didn't notice me, as I watched near by,

and all I could think of was trying to say, "Hi,"

I wanted to meet this lady so lovely,

hoping she wouldn't think badly of me...

So here I go, with what words I don't know,

a feeling like being in a silent picture

and something has fallen out of the sky and hit you,

but the words will be there,

I can feel them, there in the air...

Closer and closer to her I get,

I'm nervous and I feel sick,

but I hold on, using my nerve to keep me strong,

and with a flash of sunlight,

I can't see her; she's gone,

now I'll never get to meet her...

Lady to Cherish

Every time I see her, I get a tingle up my spine,

my heart flutters because of her,

sending romantic thoughts through my mind...

I cherish her every move,

seeing her walk, so graceful and smooth,

the touch of her hand,

light, caring, and pleasant with no demands...

Longing to know her every thought,

I look forward to listening to her,

hearing her talk,

a voice tender and sweet,

a harmony every time she speaks...

Knowing a woman such as this,

creates an everlasting yearning,

that will always exists,

in my heart and in my mind,

knowing I will love her for a lifetime...

My Love Joy

You are Beautiful as the shinning rays of the sun,

you make me look at you with wanting eyes,

you pull me in with sweetness,

the softness of your smile,

the tone of your voice,

the things that bring light to my darkened heart...

You give what I need,

I'm high by your pleasing fragrance

carried by the wind,

you make me feel home,

no matter where I may be,

the glow surrounding you flows through me...

I live with the promise of love

that will keep me close

to the space we share,

which means so very, very much...

its all about poetry

Time of Romance

The evening sun belongs to lovers,

a romantic theater of love, a setting above all others...

A time to embrace,

to grab the feeling of the moment and escape,

leaving the real world to enter fantasy,

obtaining true love and intimacy...

A wonderland, created by an energy generated between woman and man,

a potion of secrecy, a vision only lovers can see...

The perfect occasion to share feelings of the heart,

looking into the eyes of the love beautiful from the start...

My Friend

I have a friend, who is special to me,

we share a relationship that is exciting, without intimacy,

a closeness that's understood,

and that makes our friendship something good...

Our conversations are filled with variety,

being subtle and soft, or intense and fiery,

talking for hours on end,

relaying feelings and opinions we both comprehend...

I enjoy my friend for the lady she is,

a sweet person with a warm heart that gives,

I'll always cherish the times we had,

for being with her was pure class...

Love Changes

I've often wondered why people change

when in and out of love,

they never seem to be the same

once touched by Cupid's bug...

From that day of love at first sight,

to the end of it,

a lovers' quarrel or fight,

enticed by the passion of old romance,

only to be drained, giving something bad a second chance...

Going into seclusion or self-pity,

the heart that has been broken one time to many,

leaving hurt and disgust,

allowing no room for new trust...

Once again becoming an emotional independent,

not looking for love because of resentment,

living with hope for a new love,

that will be true and sent from heaven above...

Peace

The sun was bright and beaming,

as I laid in a grassy field daydreaming,

letting the warmth of the sun spread across my face,

feeling like I've discovered the perfect resting place...

Such peacefulness let's my mind be free,

allowing my dream to absorb me,

a delightful trip into wonderland,

the essence of imagination that's not hard to understand...

The light feeling of the day being more than relaxing,

becoming a time when one can find answers to questions without asking,

relishing an old freedom newly found,

through something simple as a place on the ground...

In Question

Question? Who is that courageous person

blooming with intellect and wisdom,

a true laborer and lobbyist

for family, religion, community, and the educational system...

Question? Who has provided the basic and the complex,

in terms of knowledge for survival,

giving insight to almost all situations that seem impossible,

from opinions strong and forthright,

have come the ingredients for a plausible successful life...

Question no more, for the answer is clear,

the person in question is my woman of the year,

being who and what she is, I love her,

She's my companion, she's my friend, and she's my lover...

Up and down love

Love is something hard sometimes,

the strain it puts you through can blow your mind,

it can make you feel like dying,

giving up and no-longer trying...

Love can pull your heart in all directions,

it can build you up,

then drag you down,

with all your expectations...

Love can leave you lonely when you need it most,

it can bring an empty feeling,

a feeling of lost hope...

A truly confusing factor of life, love can be,

but it shall remain the central link

between man and woman for all eternity...

its all about poetry

Wishes

Wash away the things that disturb me,

flush those feelings of heartache,

let the sidewalk of my heart be clear,

clear of the fallen leaves of love's pain...

Make me understand my emotions,

the in and outs of so called romance,

blow the gray clouds from my sky,

give me blue, the color of a new day's birth...

Widen my range of sight,

that sight which makes me look before I leap,

keep the scope of my vision focused,

so I may see the hidden dangers that lay before me...

Phase Two

Love all over

My Course

Traveling through the maze of life,

which way shall I turn,

there is no clear map that leads to promise,

I must venture into the unknown with my own course,

Though behind every corner lies an entity of danger,

I cannot be afraid nor can I hesitate,

for to reach the end safely, there must be persistence and faith...

When

When can I say I'm in love?

When can I feel that something special?

When will the pitter-patter tap at my heart?

When will I yearn for another???

When can I put my fears to rest?

When can I expose my heart?

When will I know that laughter of pleasure?

When will I see those stars of love???

Next to You

When I'm next to you

there is a chemistry that I can't explain,

a stirring within me,

that's a burning heat of emotional flames...

My body trembles when you're close,

thinking of your sensual embrace,

the thumping of my heart going faster,

as I let you take me to that special place...

Each twist, each turn, each gracious move,

are building blocks for the house of satisfaction,

where we will live for the moment,

reaching our peak together, making it everlasting...

Let's Go

Take flight with me,

explore the world of paradise,

let's find out how high we can go,

floating in a mist of love...

Help me find that secret imaginary land,

that sensation that never ends,

to know the depth of your love,

to give you all you want and more...

Together we can rule the waves of passion,

then rest the peaceful rest of lovers,

a moment of being one,

where only pleasure is king...

In Love

I really enjoyed myself the other day,

you see, I fell in love,

I stumbled into a wonderful person,

and she took me on a magical ride...

That day all my problems disappeared,

I became a part of natures many wonders,

my eyes sparkled as beauty was bestowed upon me,

I felt as if I were at the threshold of eternal happiness...

My mannerisms were altered,

I spoke in a scattered tone of excitement,

there was no control over my actions,

yet somehow, I knew everything I did was right...

Those events would replay in my thoughts,

and each new day would build a new memory,

for I've found the lady of my present and future,

that precious heart of gold...

The Lady

I had a vision in my sleep,

the image of a beautiful lady,

who looked at me with loving eyes,

sneaking into my heart in the quiet of darkness...

With poise, she moved around me,

stealing bits and pieces of my love,

she held my hand and kissed my cheek,

then surrendered to my embrace, just because...

She whispered to me softly,

those emotional over-tones so sweet,

tenderly caressing my love,

she catered to my every want and need...

My eyes fluttered and she began to fade away,

leaving me longing for her,

to bring to life our love,

to make my dream a reality...

Scared of Love

Within the shadows of my cautious heart,

there is a blaze of fear,

a haunting feeling that never leaves me,

because hurt is always near...

When I attempt to find love,

my warning lights begin to flash,

I place a fortress around my emotions,

shielding my heart fast...

I shake and shiver with each step,

as I move to a love that's new,

I take my time and hold my breath,

hoping this will be the love that's true...

Troubled

My heart is troubled,

I know not why,

a cloud of sadness shadows me,

I grieve with pain and my eyes want to cry...

I feel lonely, though I am not alone,

there is an emptiness, an open space,

I've lost that sense of love, that feeling,

my smile has been taken away...

Fault lies only with failure,

the unfulfilled dream of romance,

the vein of happiness bleeds through me,

knowing there can be no second chance...

Missing you

When I'm not with you,

all time stops,

the revolution of my world ends,

and I find myself changing...

I become consumed with my thoughts,

wanting to keep you with me,

to hold on to your pleasure,

sharing you with no one...

Even though you fill my heart,

in your absence I feel empty,

a separation of body and soul,

leaving a spirit of loneliness...

I survive only with hope,

you shall return to love me,

taking the bitterness of missing you away,

that special union of you and I once again...

Lovers Night

Last night I touched you,

I found that sacred path to your heart,

we met at a mutual point,

where our feelings became one...

I floated through a field of intimacy,

discovering uncharted areas of love,

you brought new meaning to passion,

as we entered that dimension of joy...

Oh!

Oh, when I walk with you,

such a delight to behold,

a sweet simple-ness so nice,

how could I want more...

To listen to the tender sound of your voice,

to look upon that beautiful smile,

standing with a true lady,

I know why my heart screams...

It's something utterly amazing,

and it makes sense only because of you,

my jewel, my pearl,

the one person I know I belong to...

Mercy

Look upon this soul,

there is a multitude of work and service,

undying devotion for any cause,

a triumphant soldier of glory...

Through burdens and sacrifice,

strength has come to pass,

to exalt the spirit of others,

reinforcing the power of love...

Place such a heart, of warmth and inspiration,

in the light of the divine,

that kindred body of care,

where rest shall be granted to all...

Wayward Heart

A wayward heart can travel forever

in the quest for the true feeling of love,

it can ride the wind of solitude,

until the breezing mist of another's amorous cry has come...

Though jaded by the crusade,

optimism shall never cease,

for it is the will of all hearts to find that fantasy,

to which each longs to possess...

Sensual

The touch of soft skin,

a warm caress again and again,

movements slow and in rhythm,

taking all that each has given,

together as one, a loving system,

rotating in sequence, relieving tension...

Holding, hugging, being close,

making every moment mean the most,

neglecting nothing and remembering all,

being sensitive, listening for one's name to be called,

molding inner most feelings that are true,

expressing all the things lovers do...

Spirit

Through all grief and sorrow,

always remember, there's hope for tomorrow,

even when hearts are heavy and pain severe,

still a great power is near...

With each day, keep love in your heart,

and it shall provide a fresh start,

never forget, for memories are dear,

keep them close and conquer all fear...

Pain may seem everlasting, never ending,

cycles of emotional highs and lows, extending,

forever testing, scanning the spirit,

which is the keeper of faith that leads to new beginnings...

Life and Love

New Love

Something moves deep inside,

it makes your heart want to cry,

delicate feelings that fill the soul,

heating of emotions without control...

Free spirited, spontaneous and new,

it comes so quick, there's nothing you can do,

sweet and simple, it sounds so right,

that thing called love, that happens day and night

capture it, hold it tight,

for it may be the best thing about life...

Romance

Day brings the sun, full and bright,

night brings the moon, a silver shinning light,

powers of nature that groom romantic zing,

which brings lovers close and makes hearts want to sing...

The sun, using it's morning rise,

to show the glitter in lovers' eyes,

the moon, using it's night glare,

to cast a florescent light on love affairs...

Resources like these fuel the fire of love,

that goes from heart to heart and comes from above...

Life and Love

Love Lost

Over and over, I look to my heart,

trying to remember how it was,

there had to be something,

you were the center of my love,

How can this be,

When I feel so alone and empty,

is there a chance,

can we salvage the romance...

Can we find the spark of love that comes so new,

or will it be lost, forever leaving me blue,

I will never know the secret or ever have a clue,

whatever happens, I will always love you...

Phase Three

Emotional

Fulfillment

The more I learn and understand,

I can be filled with the pleasure of you,

my defenses can descend,

allowing all emotional passion to rush in...

Saturated by the fever of love's fire,

my responses become immediate,

spontaneous to the heat created by your desire,

a needing urge to satisfy...

Willfully adhering to your sensual request,

electrifying the thoughts of what's to come,

building a monument for the moment,

to remember our embrace, all the love and fun...

When romance has found you

and taken over your heart,

you see the sparkle of a lover's smile...

When the magic of love has captured you,

a floating mist of harmony befalls the part of you once wild...

When passion's heat fills you up,

simple things become your reward,

bringing erotic feelings with the slightest touch,

drawing you closer to the one you love...

Come to Me

Please find me love,

come and save me from loneliness,

take me away from self-pity,

bring to me that feeling I've searched for,

let me see that sparkling light,

the one that lovers see when their heart is right,

that something that makes them smile,

the beautiful peace that last and last,

bind that part of me that feels so much,

so I may enjoy the essence of touch,

staying in that vine of love,

to reach the precious fruit that I adore...

Falling in Love

I've been drowning in a river of love,

the air has gone away from me,

I've reached up for the last time,

the lake of love taking me away...

My heart, has been swept by a busy stream,

dragging me down it's trail,

the pull and push of love,

driving through my heart, my world...

I've lost one life to gain another,

becoming whole leaving emptiness forever,

embracing that feeling taking control of me,

a waterfall of emotion showering my soul....

Every Now and Then

Every now and then,

I think about us,

the way we loved,

the things we shared,

the laughter that came so easily...

Every now and then,

I wonder how we lost our trust,

the belief in our feelings,

the things that mattered most for you and me...

Every now and then,

I long to love you like I use to,

holding you in that special way,

that embrace that brought more than pleasure,

Every now and then,

I ask myself, what can I do,

How can I bring you back,

can I attract the sweetness of your heart forever...

Every now and then,

has become my today and tomorrow,

for my love for you remains,

you will always be in my heart,

for my love will never change...

Finding the glory of love,

the secret that molds hearts,

is the quest for true companionship...

The path guiding toward happiness,

the road, which is endless,

leads romantic emotion,

Controlled by the mind,

what should and should not be,

confusing the feelings of the heart,

allowing attraction and stimulation to choose love,

the misconceptions of spontaneous feelings...

One Sided Love

I wanted to love her,

but she didn't want to love me,

friendship was her only interest,

I longed for intimacy...

When we were together, I felt passion,

she felt something else,

I wasn't the match she was looking for,

she'd rather be by herself...

I couldn't understand why, what was the reason,

we could have been good for each other,

the feelings I had were strong,

only she compared them to feelings of a brother...

The love I had has gone away,

but I still feel for her and I care,

she will be in my memory always,

and wherever I go she'll be there...

Circle of Passion

Everyday she passed me by; she stole my heart,

the feelings created by her presence were feelings I'd never felt before...

The air of her beauty made me die, the slow death of desire...

endlessly hoping for a chance for her love,

making me want her more and more...

Time passed ever so slowly without her,

each minute became an eternity, missing her in a lovers way,

an emptiness that could only be filled with her return...

The magical power, for which there is no answer,

bonds my mind, body, and soul,

a circle of passion ignited by that special lady,

that flame of love that will always burn...

Sad Emotion

I saw sweetness in her eyes,

a soft prettiness that came from within,

the part of her that showed me the light to her heart,

a place I know I wanted to be...

There was a passion in the air, as she talked,

it surrounded me, sending butterflies through my body,

nervously, I listened to her every word,

and I felt myself falling, losing the hold on my heart,

watching it leap from my soul to hers,

I didn't intend to let my heart open so much,

control of my emotions has always been my edge,

keeping that line drawn between like and love,

only the rush of those special feelings overcame me,

pulling at my insides, driving me to want more...

To stop the collision course to love,

I had to lock those feelings away, to be forgotten,

put to the side, to the back of my mind, gone,

never to surface again, lying deep within,

finding a loneliness, that would appear to be, Destiny...

My days will be long, my nights forever,

as I try to forget the love I have for you,

to cast those feelings far away,

hoping to survive the pain of losing you...

My strength is weakened, my heart is sad,

as my mind flickers memories of us,

thinking of what you gave to me,

that secure feeling of being loved...

My passion has gone into a slumber,

my spirit is adrift,

knowing, what was,

will never be again,

a cold emptiness I must face alone,

an eerie shadow I must get away from...

My life can only grow because of this,

my heart will mend and heal,

finding an inner peace of love,

becoming the star of my own emotions,

for pain, is something never again will I feel...

Tough love

There is a love that feels strain,

the taunt pull of another's personality,

a passive conviction to compromise,

trying to enhance the quality of a relationship...

Letting go of personal belief,

for the sake of happiness and peace,

overlooking the consciousness of one's own mind,

hoping to nurture and build on the love inside...

Such love is assumed to fuel the future,

a cascade of emotion settling into a common pool,

providing the vast amount of fulfillment longed for,

inducing that divine hope of jubilance, through monogamy...

Foreseeing what lies ahead is masked,

understanding nothing, with reasoning to inept to justify,

tightening the rein and holding the heart,

an isolation that can let the love die...

To have or have not

To wish for someone that you must have,

looking into the eyes of the one you wish for,

you hope for an acceptance that is attraction,

bringing reality and fantasy closer together...

Not understanding the magnitude of such hope,

it rest high in your mind,

searching for the magic to provoke sensuality,

the images of passion...

Vulnerable to accept what fate brings,

there's an air of anticipation,

an uneasy wait for what's to come,

a yearning urge created by your wish for new love...

Extreme Intimacy

What is it that makes us lay down,

diving into immense pleasure,

rockets of heated emotion, shooting to the sky,

the kind of feeling that last forever...

With the thoughts of sensuality,

we are drawn to an arena,

a private place of erotica,

where we are our fantasies and dreams...

Reaching and reaching, on the edge,

the taste of multiple satisfaction,

enduring until we've touched that special nerve,

opening the flood gates of lust and passion...

I Really Don't Know

Down! How did I get this way?

I don't really know,

happiness was never clear to me,

the things that made me smile

were the same things that made me frown...

Did I have a problem?

One minute I'd feel good, then the next, I'd feel bad,

it's really crazy, all a mystery to me.

Am I the only person who feels this way?

Laughing or crying, the choice should be easy,

but what do you do when one brings the other,

it's like pleasure and pain,

they both seem to mean the same thing,

Mixed up, I guess you could say so,

it's just a part of me,

the part that I really don't know...

Easy

Why can't it be easy?

Do I have to feel stress?

Can there be one day I don't have to be at my best?

Why can't it be easy?

I want to relax and kick back,

instead of being on my Ps and Qs; always on the attack...

Why can't it be easy?

Life's just to short,

it ought to be fun just like a game, a sport...

Why can't it be easy?

a question we all ask,

but something easy always turns out hard and kicks our   ...

Dream Girl

He dialed her phone number and waited,

with each ring his heart jumped and danced,

would she answer, would she be there,

he was so excited he couldn't sit or stand...

Getting her number had been a chore,

taking every bit of his nerve to ask,

she was his dream-girl, someone he could adore,

it was the type of feeling that would always last...

Anticipation was building as he listened to the third ring,

an impatience that drained all of his hope,

he wanted to hang up but realized that would be mean,

so he waited on the fourth ring almost at the end of his rope...

Then there was a click, as if someone answered the line,

he was ready, he knew what he was going to say,

but before he could speak, a voice sang out, "call back some other time,"

so ended his chance to talk to his dream-girl today...

The Affair

The covers fell to the floor,

the bed rolled and rocked,

time became suspended for this affair,

the tumble of love for the moment...

It was suppose to be hot,

Exciting, because there was no meaning,

just the hit and run of an exciting high,

to grab that physical sensation and hold it for a minute...

And, as the intense heat builds so quickly,

it sub-sides even quicker, almost a flash,

the mechanisms of the interlude, desiccate and flaccid,

introducing the score keeper of the game with points, good or bad...

But the scorekeeper holds no merit,

for as the last garment has covered the flesh,

so closes the house of pleasure, re-opening the world of pain,

and the search for that life long sensation, "Love", begins once again...

The Theater

Two lovers argued about their feelings,

anger swept into the theater of their love,

it became the star of their differences...

The first performance donned the male ego,

a rough exterior with no need to show emotion,

"I am a man!," was the sentiment,

to show no vulnerability, only strength...

The contrast came with the portrayal of women's' intuition,

the unmistakable keen sense of foresight,

deep seeded sensors of perception,

through the tentacles of love stretched so far...

Act after act, scene after scene,

anger was efficacious, capturing the persona of both characters,

so much so, that anger became more than a player,

it became the show, the stage, the arena, the den of lions...

The lovers soon found nothing to say,

for anger had consumed them whole,

which brought silence, the adversary to anger,

opening the door, closing the theater with love...

To Love Another

I can't understand sometimes,

when you give of yourself totally,

to be there for another's call,

and not receive in kind...

When you display the qualities of affection,

that are tools for lasting love,

taken lightly by an unknowing heart,

you feel as if you're waiting at the end of the line...

To be ready when the chips fall,

lending your shoulder and listening ear,

hoping one day the light will shine,

and they're realize love has always been there...

But we're not always given what we want,

those who hold our hearts are not those who give us love,

we see, we hear, and we know,

yet, we never surrender because what's inside is really love...

Time passes and we move on, but never forget,

a part of us remains with that person,

that lost harmony within, shared by someone else,

forever living life with a tinge of regret...

Refusing to Die

I've stood in the fields of misery to long,

my time has come to pass,

to commit to me, my life,

to be pushed, stepped on, no more...

Let no beauty shade my eyes,

let no lust or physical attraction sway me,

for my focus must be internal,

placing my spirit first...

No man, no beast, no evil,

shall steal my hope or my courage,

I will be the victor,

a body of distinction, shinning in a clad of armor.

The land upon which I walk will be mine,

high stepping with a purple heart across my chest,

for I carry the scars of a wounded heart,

the heart that refuses to die...

Door for Dreams

There is a knock at my front door,
I walk slowly to see who's there,

but it appears no one is there,
I look frantically around to be sure,

my nerves reek havoc with my mind,
I'm scared now; I feel a chill,

a ghostly win howling only at my door,
it blows harder and harder,

I can feel my skin pulled tightly against my face,
the wind's power increases, swooping in on me,

tears flood my eyes,
tragedy has embarked around me,

isolated to be at the mercy of my fate,
or what I will accept,

for it must be me who closes the door,
shutting out the rushing air that damages my dreams,

but dreams of life rely on the wind,
they float to carry us to our destiny,

no, the door will not be closed,
I must be the shield and protector of my dreams,

cultivating the wind, conquering fear,
converting this eminent danger to opportunity,

for those dreams sheltered and unexposed, are dreams never pursued,
they don't catch the wave and so they fade,

the door never opens and dreams are locked away...

No Patience for Success

The clock strikes twelve, it's mid-day,

another morning gone with no progress,

the TV has been the alternative to dead time,

being the one thing that doesn't turn against you...

The morning paper has been disappointing,

once again, sifting through a rubble of adds for a maybe,

a one shot chance to start fresh,

to rebuild a house of non-existent stability...

Tension still rains thunderous drops of anger,

left behind from the early morning's quarrel,

a sad ritual born during the tough times,

times created by untimely misfortune...

With bills mounting and no moral support,

animosity grows to heights never seen,

constructing a large wall of resistance and rejection

that no one can begin to scale...

Thus, the ones we love and depend on

become the ones we hate and run from,

simply because patience for success is absent,

that key ingredient for any plausible commitment...

Finding Myself

One day I woke up and I was blind,

it felt as though I were under a spell,

I walked in a direction unfamiliar to me,

never really going where I wanted to go...

Unconsciously, I waltzed to a song I hated,

my arms entwined with a mere void,

I listened but could hear no sound,

a quiet that brought a sadness into my heart...

The castle in my dreams no longer belongs to me,

I pass through it's halls only a visitor,

an apparition locked within a span of misery,

searching for it's soul...

Conclusions of my pain restored my sight,

the tears within drove me forward with courage,

learning to live for my own music,

dancing with true peace and joy...

Street Corner

She stood on the busy street corner,

not knowing that my eyes were upon her,

watching her every move on that street,

made my pulse race and my heart beat...

I wanted to shout her name, but I was afraid,

being shy and feeling shame,

for her beauty was so stunning so rare,

I didn't have the courage to talk to her,

all I could do was stare...

It seemed like an eternity watching her stand there,

as crowds of people moved around her everywhere,

I wanted to go to her, tell her how I felt,

but the coward in me held me back causing my heart to melt...

Time began to go faster as she left her space,

moving away from me and the corner at a furious pace,

my heart fell to the bottom of my soul and I didn't know what to do,

for I was letting her walk away, and with her, my dream too...

Goodbye

My hand shakes,

my heart aches,

I'm dying slow, as I watch you go.

Yesterday you discovered something new,

the person you love has been untrue,

anger rushes through your veins,

as your heart tries to fight the pain...

There's nothing to say that could make you stay,

love has gone because I was wrong,

for you, happiness awaits,

true love is your fate...

For me this is the end,

I've left you searching for revenge,

a feeling that teases and never really allows any peace,

you will be satisfied and start to love again,

My love has been lost and so has my best friend...

Just for You

What can I say ?

What can I do?

That is special and just for you...

I can tell you that you're beautiful,

I can say that you're fine,

but most of all,

I can tell you that you're always on my mind...

I can shower you with compliments,

conveying my thoughts again and again,

I can let you see my affection,

the hunger that comes from within...

Like Cupid Shooting an arrow,

I'll penetrate your heart,

a blazing flash of romance,

I'll make you ignite and spark...

A passion no one else can see,

simplistic paradise full of ecstasy,

what we share will always be,

a sensual secret between you and me...

Lady True-Love

There is a mystery about you,

a story quietly stealing the hearts of men,

the shadow of your beauty

slowly drains the power to resist,

the presence of your burning eloquence...

A brush of your hand feels like a night's sea breeze,

stroking the shores of a lovers' beach,

you twinkle the stars as you fill midnight dreams,

the power you possess is a sight unseen...

You are the picture of a thousand brides,

men marry you and lose themselves,

induced by your sweet seduction,

you are the barer of life,

the reason men fall, and why love exist,

you are Lady True-Love...

A True Lady

Like roses that bloom in the spring,

you are soft and sweet,

an array of beautiful things,

a heart that is an overflowing fountain of love,

always open to the one your fond of...

Being with you is like heaven on earth,

refreshing and awakening,

a feeling of rebirth,

a comfort beyond all fantasy,

forever wonderful and pleasing to me...

With compassion, your heart is always filled,

warm and sincere, always real,

overlooking the short comings that I have,

becoming my support, my staff...

Being all that any man could want,

a true lady with qualities that are natural and can't be taught,

a love that comes only once in a life time,

the one true lady who's all mine...

Storage of Love

There is a grace that exists between you and I,

a secure feeling we share as we face obstacles in our lives...

Something you and I can draw from when needed,

a support base of emotional power that cannot be depleted...

Sponsored by a devotion to true commitment,

an exchange of inner feelings with no resentment...

What we possess is a spirit of care,

our hearts, a storage of love that will always be there...

Life and Love

Will of Your love

Can you imagine what you've done,

you've opened up a world I never knew,

I've found an ecstasy that didn't exist,

feelings brought on by being in your arms....

My mind has been set free,

only to be captured again,

let go by the thrill you bring,

restrained by the need for your pleasure...

I've entered the land of never,

because your sweetness is eternal,

the touch of your hand, a magic,

a will of love, I could only hope to return...

Special Love

You are like a flower to me,

beautiful, soft, and sweet,

your heart is like a rainbow,

colors together, enchanted, complete...

Your skin is smooth to the touch,

your body a temple of grace,

sensual is your feeling,

always the right time and place...

Your love is tender and gentle,

compromising and sentimental,

giving is your nature, honest and true,

always helping others less fortunate than you,

a vision of loveliness is what you are,

in my eyes, a heavenly star...

Life and Love

My true love

Something surrounds me,

it holds me and caresses me,

my eyes fill with tears,

yet, all sadness disappears...

I feel warm and secure,

like I've found my lost home,

the world seems so bright and clear,

a peace I could never have alone...

My life has been embraced,

I live for tomorrow, because of what we have today,

true love has finally come my way...

Love Me

Sing me a love song,

open your heart and let me in,

show me your private thoughts,

and be with me like no other...

Seduce me with your fantasy,

fuel the fire in my soul,

I want to caress every fiber of your being,

the human essence of your love...

Give me your all,

as I will give to you,

let us visit paradise,

if only for a moment or too...

Beauty

Beauty, where can it be?

Is there any out there for me?

I feel like a child, waiting in line for candy,

getting to the front of the line with no candy left for me.

Have I been overlooked?

Has nature failed?

Have I been robbed of my fairy tale?

My heart waits in quite hibernation,

until the warmth of beauty shadows me,

a cast of love formed with elegance and glamour...

Morning After

A comforter hangs off the side of the bed,

sheets are rumpled and torn,

articles of clothing cover the floor and room,

as if they'd never been worn...

The smell of lust lingers from the heat of unyielding passion,

the remains of a physical encounter,

packed with emotional explosions and sensual blasting...

Empty prophylactic containers rest on the nightstand,

packaging ripped to shreds,

laced underwear, split in half, lay alone in the middle of the bed...

Everything left behind,

almost on display,

all the telling signs of the way lovers play...

Good Love

So good! So good!

I feel like running rapids are rushing through me,

gigantic waves slam against my heart...

The freshness of spring water fills my spirit,

while the fountain of youth sprinkles me with cool rain drops,

I have the world at bay, my passage is clear,

trouble, I leave behind,

for my feeling brings no fear...

Mountains recede to molehills,

for an easy glide of joy,

I have the strength of the sun,

the glow of the moon,

I feel like a child with a new toy...

Lover

I like the feel of you,

the close embrace,

I'm always in the mood,

just to get into your space...

That atmospheric zone where I get lost,

keeps me coming, back,

again and again to sheer exhaust...

In you, is where I find my peace,

nothing and no one can harm me,

my emotions are set off when I'm in your arms,

and that's when I reach my extremity...

My Daydream

I'm having another daydream,

and it's all about you,

my mind is taking me on a journey,

a spiraling maze I can't get though...

I see you, a shadowy silhouette,

your body is so beautiful,

my eyes light up and my mouth gets wet,

it's like a special treat I haven't had yet...

I imagine my hand yearning to touch,

a part, a place, a little piece,

I stretch and grab but it's not enough,

you're still well beyond my reach...

As your image starts to fade,

I know it's almost the end,

my mind has given me brief ecstasy,

lasting visions of you until my daydream comes again...

Love Life

I don't want to grow up to fast!

I want to remember what it means to be young,

to live care free with a light attitude,

enjoying every waking moment,

for the years pass without knowing,

the days run away from you

and you wonder where they went.

Time is a precious gem,

one that is priceless and uncontrollable,

what little there is has to be valued.

I don't want to look up one day and I'm old

not realizing a lifetime has come and gone,

leaving me reaching back for wants that can never be.

I want to do all that can be done in this life,

for to wait and wait is to lose and miss,

letting a sunny day pass by, doing nothing,

wishing for it when the rain comes,

holding back because of disappointment and failures,

becoming over protective, overlooking real joy and pleasure,

my philosophy is simple, live full for the here and now,

let today be the day you love life...

The Formula

Look deep when you search for love,

go beyond the outward surface,

pursue that root of another's soul that's true,

to know where their heart lies,

Give way to spontaneous reaction,

but commit to real feelings,

allowing room for exploration,

the trial and error of relationships,

Say yes to those propositions that merit consideration,

say no to proposals filled with false words,

give love when you feel love,

for no one is immune to the decease heartbreak...

Life and Love

Secret

Give me the hidden secret,

the golden words spoken lightly,

to ease my way slowly into you...

I want to bring you the feeling you're accustom too,

the one that pleases your needs,

and satisfies all of your fantasies...

With me, gentle strokes of love you shall have,

lasting sensations that stimulate your thoughts,

arriving in paradise, where nothing will be lost...

The Gift

Being wrapped up with you is the gift of all gifts,

to touch every part of you,

a simple sweet preciousness...

I thirst for the taste of your love,

that is burning fiery hot,

waiting until that moment of no return,

to release all the love I've got...

Let no time be wasted,

give me the pleasures of your feeling,

the deepest center of something good,

a place I know I'll love being....

The Presence of You

The life within me

lives by the presence of you,

that string of feeling

running in and out, all around my heart...

I've welcomed your touch,

to be your bond,

that driving support of warmth,

to be close to you...

We've turned simple pleasures

into moments of memories,

those romantic times together,

creating daydreams that never end...

My Thoughts

Swing with me,
I'm looking for a partner to get into,

my appetite is getting out of control,
give me the joy that only you hold...

Hark, I hear the sound of a pulsating heart,
it's beating vigorously with anticipation,

there's an echo with each rhythmic phase,
chambers and valves flexing in constant rotation,

the rush of adrenaline enhancing the performance of it's special power...
I can feel the spasms going through your body,

I can taste the sweetness of your juices,
my heart beats frantically, as I await your love,

I am your victim, I am your hero,
together we will experience a sensual treasure...

The thoughts that enter my mind
are exciting interludes that I share with you,

we dance to a slow song and hold each other close,
we dine and sip fine wine, drifting pleasantly in a romantic ocean...

Space and time have no meaning when I experience these feelings,
I see only the color of your eyes, pure and clear,

I feel your heart beat steady and strong,
my attraction to you is like honey to a bee,

a part of you has been stapled inside of me,
a bond that will not release or brake,

Rings of sensitivity encircle me,
Because of you, I rest in a fortress of paradise...

Life and Love

Oh Lady!

Oh Lady! I can't stop looking at you,

your lips are so tantalizing,

your smile is so appetizing,

put them together and you're mesmerizing,

your eyes gleam as you gaze my way,

your body language says things I'd never say,

the vibes come strong from the depths of your passion,

I'd give you the world without you even asking...

Oh Lady! I can't stop looking at you,

your hips are slippery tight,

your cloths are always perfect, just right,

the power of you could give a blind man sight,

your spirit floats through my body,

I know I've got to fight for control,

you can awaken the strength in any man, young or old,

and patience, it's not a virtue when you are around,

my blood rushes, because with you I want to be down...

Oh Lady! I can't stop looking at you,

your sweet voice is like a picture,

your intelligence wraps you up and grips you,

taking sensuality to a level I've never seen before,

you bring the whole package,

sexuality, intellect, compassion and more...

its all about poetry

I want

I have a ferocious urge

that's boiling and brewing inside,

a craving for something hot, sweet, and sticky,

that does more that satisfy...

I want to know that fire,

I want to feel that flame,

let me ease into the garden, open and wild,

and extract it's juices like saccharine from sugarcane...

If the fruit is forbidden,

then I must falter and take a bite,

for my want and need remain extreme,

I will plunge into the abyss of a love filled night,

floating, as if I were a cherry on top of cool whipped cream...

Life and Love

It's Over

Just the other day I was so in love with you,

now, I can't say that I feel the same way for you,

I'm talking about bad love,

the kind that makes you feel so sad...

I guess it was all the pain,

coming in and out of our lives,

we couldn't stand the rain,

we couldn't make it right...

Now that it's come to an end,

it feels so strange,

I thought we would always be friends,

and now I can hardly mention your name,

I'm talking about bad love,

the kind that makes you feel so mad...

Knowing that it's over makes me realize,

you've got to be more than lovers,

if a love is ever to survive...

Timid About Love

I thought I was in love once long ago,

I had that inner joy that only love can bring,

my smile was always alive,

everyday became another day of pleasure...

I didn't see the pain that was coming,

I didn't know love was going to be so cruel,

taking my heart and squeezing it to it's breaking point,

forever rendering my heart tender...

Now my trust of others is limited,

I find it hard to release the misery of my past,

even with new experiences, I drift back somehow,

back to the charade of a love never meant to be...

I know I'll love again someday,

that is the beauty of life,

but the lessons I've learned have been hard,

leaving me a hopeless romantic who is timid about love...

Lovers

From two different worlds they came,

variety for the enhancement of new found love,

free hearts merging to form meaningful feelings,

deeply lodged in a pre-planned relationship unknown...

Even though they'd loved before,

the uninhibited emotions present made this one exceptional,

a breakthrough in the ever existing research of true love,

they were pioneers, uncovering the mystery of soul mates,

lust and attraction held no importance in the beginning,

for there was no awareness of the love concealed...

Yet, as they were drawn together,

an unyielding passion evolved,

constructing a pyramid of devotion towering into the heavens,

a temple of commitment,

to praise the blessings of what they shared,

accepting the greatest gift, real love...

Life and Love

The Ultimate Peak

A silent voice speaks to the heart,

it whispers those words of stimulation,

the secrets, the hidden pleasures,

the things that reveal themselves on the heels of romance,

coming to life with fire,

they dance to build the tingle of the mind,

while the breath of excitement flows in an out,

quivering motions and uncontrolled movements,

a sea of love,

splashing thoughts in a storm,

breaking free to open the doors of amour,

a whimsical spin,

turning and turning,

intensifying the warmth within,

climbing toward the ultimate peak,

the place where the vein is beautiful,

where the eyes can see the magic...

its all about poetry

Easy to Love

It is easy to love,

to throw the peddles of roses in the pond of your love garden,

showing the beauty of your heart...

Yet, it is not easy to love,

to look in the reflection of another's' eyes,

and know the music plays,

but it is not your song that is heard...

It is easy to love,

to give unconditionally,

becoming the gift of the one who awakens every fiber of your soul,

a word, a glance, a simple touch...

Yet it is hard to find love,

to hope that attraction will come,

that the diamond within you will capture their desire,

working endlessly to impress,

offering your sweetest nectar to tempt their taste...

It is easy to love, the one that loves you....

Momentary Recluse

Standing in the middle of my room,

there's a quiet place,

an isolation from everyone and everything,

an area of space only I can enter...

The walls don't close in on me,

because my mind is free,

I'm restrained by nothing,

I can explore any dimension...

The things that appear complex,

now take form to become simple,

resolve is at the very front,

an evaluation of what is vital...

Peace bears an essence of what's real,

a momentary recluse,

addressing concerns about life,

a conscious, yet hypnotic state,

where answers flow from a source,

which can only be heavenly...

No Peace

Peace comes to those who are at peace with themselves.

Although, the complexities of one's persona are extreme,

it easy to be lost, consumed by the enormous pressures of worry.

Pointless affection to shield this worry is dangerous.

Severe damage to one's self-confidence can occur.

Hiding never produces an answer to one's difficulties,

solving problems bridged on fantasy,

reciting faults in others rather that addressing one's own faults.

Fleeing into seclusion is always an easy alternative,

an escape route to dash away from the existing problem,

which can cause emotional indecisiveness,

leaning toward one idea or feeling, then backing away in a hurry,

a fear of making the wrong decision.

Thus creating a feeling that you are missing something in life,

building paranoia, an affixation to find that one thing,

that one person, that one feeling or love,

to pull all the pieces of the puzzle together.

The pieces will fit but the picture won't be true,

for the search to find that perfection will have flawed the mind.

The once found quick-fix illusory love will become imperfection,

which will devastate, frustrate, and almost break the spirit...

Life and Love

New Beginnings

Wake up!

Pull back the covers,

today is the day you find yourself a new lover,

no more drips or dips,

no more flips or flops,

what you want is

someone to make your heart zip, roar, and rock,

no all-night party freaks or self-righteous fouls,

you want someone nice and neat, laid back, and real cool,

time to get the party started, yesterday is old news,

the morning sun represents new beginnings with one rule,

love yourself before you try to love someone else...

Her Time

She ignored the voices of her children,

closed out the demands of her husband,

scolded the dog as she removed him from the house,

then settled into the confines of a bath...

The water soothed her aches and eased her mind,

her only escape from the rigors of family,

trading places with her troubles for a moments peace,

that single period of solitude that was her own...

She shared nothing here,

nothing could penetrate her palace,

for her dreams stood constant guard,

pushing away whatever reality existed...

The knock on the door was not acknowledged,

the calling of her name, a faint sound,

she possessed the power of silence,

to enjoy the time when she could finally be alone...

The fantasy last only a short while,

for as the water drains away she's back home,

to restore order and bring back life,

being that vein of support, wife and mom...

Lonely Hearts

The chase and hunt,

it's a game played by lonely hearts,

the seekers of courtship,

lusting for the idealistic love of their dreams...

Some give in to pursuit,

others fight and evade the inevitable,

but ultimately surrender to harmonic need,

releasing mystical fantasies of romance,

seemingly that final quest of being in love...

Hiding

We often hide from the truth,

the plain facts of what we need,

we stand firm to express our independence,

our personal emotional stability,

knowing that there is a part of us that cries,

that part, which is vulnerable,

wanting to share our inner feelings,

to know that we are understood and cared for...

We yearn for compatibility,

that special someone who brings happiness,

that solid foundation to help withstand difficulties,

those periods in life when support is a necessity,

We establish a resistance to our needs,

therefore, moving on with life,

letting the memories of love pacify our heart...

Life and Love

Twisted and Turned

For to many days

I've seen the bitterness that comes with the strain of working for love,

I've watched anxiety build and explode

in the souls of those who bare the burden,

constantly maintaining a balance of frustration and anger,

with confused attitudes, adjusted and changed,

what's left behind are flustered minds with boiling hearts,

twisted and turned, allowing only turmoil to remain...

When I Walk Alone

When I walk alone,

I see the world for what it is,

my conscious becomes a silent narrator,

patiently explaining those things that I see,

When I walk alone,

I feel spiritually strong,

a power that exists because of my faith,

the source that tells me why I belong,

When I walk alone,

I know no fear,

for bravery encompasses my soul,

my direction comes from the heavens,

When I walk alone,

I am trouble free,

for with each step I take,

there is a higher power walking right beside me...

Life and Love

We Share Love

Listen to the morning sounds,

you turn to me and I start to come around,

You whisper "good morning," oh so good,

I hold you and say, " I love you," then,

You reach out for me and hold me for what seems like eternity...

As we enjoy heavens gift, we feel the pleasure, oh so quick,

the music of midnight still plays,

feelings flowing, building passions of love,

carrying our hearts forward in the direction of happiness...

We arrive hand in hand, arm in arm,

we need no formula for love,

the myth that love never comes easy, faintly emerges,

a scary fable from those who never learn how to love,

and we stay strong uniting our souls to become one,

leaving no question, we share love...

Nothing Left

Somewhere along the way,

I lost my love for you,

there's no one to blame,

it's just something I'm going through...

I guess we never found that magic that lovers share,

I wish I could turn it around,

because I know that I still care...

But love don't give no guaranties,

it can build you up then bring you to your knees,

Love don't give no guaranties,

but it's the one feeling that will set you free...

I said I'd never leave you,

I promised you my heart,

but I'm not going to deceive you,

our love has fallen apart...

Maybe the day will come,

and I'll know that I made a mistake,

letting your love go is a chance I'll just have to take...

Life and Love

Love....lucky

All this crying and whining has got me upset,

I don't need the aggravation of this nonsense,

love and romance, you got to be kiddin me,

that kind of thing only exist in the movies and on TV,

Nobody really cares about romance,

they want to look good and prance,

got to get paid,

it's the center, that old dollar bill,

the hustler's game,

that's all it is,

You got to check it out from all sides,

you'll be bouncing and jamming and won't know why,

got these superficial material possessions,

manipulating the mind and keeping it away from the spirit,

yea, that's right, the spirit of your soul,

the storage facility for your emotional ammunition,

an arsenal of strong feelings constantly on patrol,

better take a minute to really see,

there's a whole world out there wondering, love...lucky...

Things happen at the blink of an eye,

chance is opportunity waiting in the wings,

I'm moved by people I can feel,

I can look into their heart and know the whole deal,

Life and Love

It's a game, sure, that's the ticket.

But it's your turn at the plate,

What ya gonna do? Live or die, sink or swim!

This is the part where I grab the line and reel on in,

for I see the passion in failed love affairs,

it motivates me to love again,

to open up those feelings of new love once more,

to experience the first few moments of love's joy,

I know being lucky is having and sharing love...

Coming Releases
From

<u>Montgomery Productions</u>

Back and Fourth, a Poetic Love Story

By Michael Montgomery Matthews and Glynis Rhodes

Think for a Minute

By Michael Montgomery Matthews

Circle of Blame

By Michael Montgomery Matthews